Praise for *The Spring of Hope*

The Spring of Hope by Carolyn Cobelo touches the heart of the matter—the hidden Mary in every one of us. In these profound communications Mary introduces us to the hierarchies of angels, and guides us along the wave of force now entering the Earth's energy field. Miracles are revealed, and you are led to see that you are the greatest miracle of all.

Carolyn Cobelo lives the truths that Mary has given her. She is a lady avatar appointed to offer profound love to all. Through agonizing suffering and heartbreak, she has continued to move forward with her great service to Mary and the universal principles of light. I would not consider my library complete without every one of her books. She is love, and the pages of her books reveal her depth of love for us all.

—Carol B. Knight
Author of *Passing the Torch: The Way of the Avatar*

The Spring of Hope is a beautiful and gentle book that brings us guidance and hope for living our greatest potential in the coming millennium. Mary's voice comforts us as she speaks about living with angels, handling change, communicating truth, understanding our relationship with money, overcoming through love, living beyond computers, and experiencing miracles. Her ultimate message is to put our faith and trust in God, and then in ourselves. Through this book we feel Mary's presence in our hearts, strengthening us and giving us the courage to transform our feelings of unworthiness and to live life with passion and purpose.

—Jayn Stewart
Editor, spiritual counselor, and teacher

The Spring of Hope is a truly inspired and inspiring work! Carolyn Cobelo has brought forth an offering of love and wisdom, providing the reader with a deeper and broader understanding of life as an evolutionary journey of love back to oneness with the divine, while making us aware of the unconditionally loving guidance and support continuously available to us.

A "must read" for any and all of us who seek love, peace, truth, and hope.

—Layla J. H. Davis-Oakland
Spiritual counselor and teacher

Also by Carolyn E. Cobelo:

The Power of Sacred Space: Exploring Ancient Ceremonial Sites

Awakening to Soul Love: Pathways to Intimacy

Twenty-Five Power Places

Avalon: The Temple of Connection
A Game of Spiritual Transformation

THE SPRING OF HOPE

THE SPRING OF HOPE

Messages
from Mary

Carolyn E. Cobelo

AKASHA PRODUCTIONS
Santa Fe, New Mexico

Published by
Akasha Productions
223 N. Guadalupe, Suite 402
Santa Fe, New Mexico 87501

Editor: Ellen Kleiner

Book design and production: Marilyn Hager

Cover art, design, and production: Ivan Castillo

Cover image: *Pietà* c. 1499 by Michelangelo

A Blessingway book

Printed in the United States of America
on acid-free recycled paper

Mary, Blessed Virgin, Saint (Spirit)
    Spring of hope : messages from Mary /
[channeled] by Carolyn E. Cobelo. -- 1st ed.
        p. cm.
        LCCN: 99-72133
        ISBN: 0-9670412-1-X

    1. Mary, Blessed Virgin, Saint (Spirit)--
Prophecies--Miscellanea. 2. Spirit writings.
3. Twenty-first century--Forecasts. 4. Spiritual
life--New Age movement. 5. Technology--Moral and
ethical aspects.   I. Cobelo, Carolyn E.
II. Title.

BF1311.M42C63 2000   133.9'3
                                        QBI99-761

            10 9 8 7 6 5 4 3 2 1

This book is dedicated to
my beloved mother and father,
who gave me life and the foundation
of nurturance that enabled me to receive
Mary's love and compassion.

With gratitude to:

My beloved companion Mary, who transmitted this book through me. I thank you from the depths of my heart for sharing your love and presence throughout my life, and for aligning with me so that I could be your messenger;

My belated husband Esteban E. Cobelo, who shared most of this journey with me. Thank you for struggling so hard to believe in Mary, and for trusting her presence in your travels with me through the veils of life after death;

My beloved children, Nicole, Tonya, and Sophie Rousmaniere, who accepted, supported, and loved me as I ventured into realms of existence that were bizarre in the eyes of conventional society. Thank you for being brave enough to share this voyage with me and to trust that your crazy mother had some method to her madness;

My spiritual counselors, Layla Oakland, Judy Fisher, Carmella Rappozzo, and Verna Yater, who provided the foundation of support and guidance that enabled me to step into my trust and faith in Mary as a spiritual guide. Thank you for seeing me as the messenger and embodiment of the goddess energy when I could not see or accept this in myself;

My students and clients who, through their trust and love, evoked the magical voice and hands of Mary that passed through me to them. Thank you for believing in me and trusting the guidance and healing energy that Mary transmitted to you.

CONTENTS

PREFACE

ary is the Great Mother, the Great Goddess, the Queen of Heaven, the Jewel in the Lotus. She glows with the light of God. Each time I see her, her gown shimmers in brilliant luminescent colors of blue, green, orange, and pink. Her crown of magnificent peacock-blue feathers reaches high into the heavens, disappearing into the dark velvet void of emptiness. Her voice, in quiet repose, reflects the secret of God's love. Her deep gold eyes shine with the beauty of the universe, and her golden skin glows with the light of love. Her companion is the owl, reflected in the shape of her face. Her compassion is God's compassion. She holds the scepter of holy matrimony, the wand of God.

She has many names, many forms. She is the one from whom all else emerges. She is the mother of Jesus. She is also an angel and she is an expression of God as the Mother of God. A great feminine spirit, she has incarnated both as man and woman upon the Earth. She provides healing, balancing, and comfort. She's the feminine expression of God—God in the material form. She is the Mother Goddess.

Throughout Earth's history, she has assumed many archetypal forms: Inanna, Astarte, Asherah, Arnath, Demeter, Mother Nature, Cybele, Tara, Quan Yin, Isis, Shakti, Radha, Gaia. Several of her names have been lost in the currents of time. She is the healing hand of God and the vehicle for the will of God. She comes on the blue ray of light, represented in art by the color blue. When we align our consciousness with hers, we can see her as a brilliant spark of blue light, known as the Blue Pearl, shining in space. She carries souls to birth and she greets souls at death. She radiates compassion, unconditional love, non-judgment, wisdom, guidance, comfort, peace, trustworthiness, joyfulness, and knowing.

What is Mary's role? It is to take us to God, to teach us about God, to share her compassion and unconditional love, to comfort and heal us, to be a bridge between the worlds, to initiate us at birth and death, and to bring peace on Earth.

Mary is the eternal spring of hope, offering her waters of compassion, love, and acceptance for us to bathe in. As we allow her presence to permeate our consciousness and fill our hearts, we find the courage and strength to face and transform our feelings of unworthiness. Her enveloping waters support and inspire us to open to the desire for true love and to clear the pathway to this love by learning how to know, love, and accept ourselves. She leads us through the treacherous forest of self-delusion and self-judgment. She guides us to love and comfort our inner children, who suffered as we traversed the crossroads of life.

She is the primordial waters from which all else evolves, and yet in her manifested form she cares for and protects us each individually. She awakens us to life after death and heals our fear of separation. She gives us the will to live and to seek God in our hearts.

Although she is continually present for us as a source of guidance, assistance, comfort, and love, we may resist receiving her into our hearts. Old conditioning and fears of unworthiness, abandonment, judgment, inadequacy, and loss of freedom can obstruct the realization of our direct connection to her. However, this book will assist you in opening to her presence with ease, freedom, and peace, for the words contain her vibration. You will feel this vibration most profoundly by reading her messages out loud.

Because I do not always consciously feel her presence when I begin to connect to her in meditation, I often ask, "Are you there, Mary?" She always answers, "I am here, my child." She usually ends her messages with an invitation: "Call upon me and I shall be there." Reading her words on the following pages will activate your call to her. How you respond is up to you. I can only say that the more you open to her, the more she will guide and assist you in your personal and spiritual growth.

How do I know Mary? My early religious training was in the Unitarian Church. There I learned that God was nature, and that Mary and Jesus were great human beings. There was no mention of spirits or angels as participants in our everyday existence.

As an adult, I explored spirituality first through the teachings of Siddha Yoga, which was brought to the United States by a Hindu guru, Swami Muktananda, in the early 1970s. During my four years of study with Muktananda, the force of spiritual energy, known in this Indian tradition as Kundalini, burned through my subtle nervous system. It manifested as visions, dances, speaking in ancient languages, loud screams, shaking, classical Hindu dream images, yogic postures, unfamiliar tongue movements, exotic tastes, and sexual passion. I learned to surrender my ego to the will of the guru who represented an expression of my own inner self. I loved Muktananda as my spiritual father, and I was devastated when he died in 1982. His death served as a catalyst for my study of spiritual healing and channeling.

My first spiritual guide was Zarathusthra, founder of the Zoroastrian religion. He replaced Muktananda as my spiritual father and was with me from 1983 to 1988, healing my relationship to the masculine, which included my inner male, the men in my family, and the men with whom I'd had loving relationships. Zarathusthra guided me in my practice of spiritual healing and psychotherapy. He taught me Zoroastrian-inspired spiritual practices and dances, which I formed into Atar fire ceremonies. His unconditional love and understanding helped me pass through difficult transitions in my life with relative ease. I loved him with all my heart, learning that the more I opened to his love, the more wisdom and support I received.

Zarathustra presented himself to me, in an image of light, as an older man with silver hair and beard, and bright, sparkly blue eyes. He was dressed in a long robe with vertical stripes of different colors and a round, Muslim-looking hat. The clarity of his presence evolved over several years as I adjusted to his vibrational force and accepted him as a reality in my life. It was only near the end of our active relationship that I could see him fully with my third eye.

Zarathustra was born in Airyaneem-Vaejah, in the region of Bactria in eastern Iran. The date of his birth is not known, although scholars tend to agree that it was between 1400 and 1200 B.C. When he was a young man, he had visions and began communicating with Ahura Mazda, who later became the supreme spirit of the Zoroastrian religion. Inspired by these experiences, he won over the king and queen of his region, and began fervent missionary work that extended into India and China.

I knew nothing of Zarathustra or the Zoroastrian religion when I began my communication with him. Then after two years, I realized it would be helpful to know about him as a living man. I found the research so fulfilling that I named my healing center Ahura Mazda Institute. As time passed, I remembered a previous lifetime in which I was a warrior with a dark brown metal helmet and chest armor, living very close to Zarathustra, as a brother and protector. Now, when I feel his presence again, tears of love well up in my eyes, and time and space disappear.

In 1988 I began to feel a feminine presence close to me. Over the next three years this presence grew stronger, and Zarathusthra's guidance faded into the background. When I finally asked for her name in 1991, she answered, "I am Mary." I did not speak her name publicly for about two years, because I was afraid of an adverse reaction. Finally, when I realized that I was worthy of bringing her voice into the world, I revealed her name. To my surprise, most people were delighted to know that Mary was with them. Using me as a channel, she has since healed bodies and souls in many places around the world, and I have grown to accept her presence as a reality in my life.

Mary came to me physically for the first time in April 1991 at Iguaçu Falls, located at the intersection of Brazil, Argentina, and Paraguay, and considered one of the seven natural wonders of the world. I was feeling sad and lonely as I sat beside the thunderous waters of the falls. I closed my eyes in meditation. Suddenly, I felt a powerful, comforting, healing, loving presence surround me. Love seemed to be coming out of the air, and I was floating in a cloud of love. It was a real physical experience, as if someone very large were wrapping me in a blanket of love. When I opened my eyes, the pain and loneliness were gone and my heart was light, open, and free.

Mary responds directly to prayer. The answers to my prayers are not always what I expect, but I have learned that they are in my best interest and that of everyone else involved. My prayers to her have helped me in my relationships with men, my children, my family, my students, my friends, my colleagues, and my advisors. She has created clarity amid confusion, indecision, and fear. She has healed my body, spirit, and soul, and has comforted me in times of despair. She has laughed with me, gently teasing and joking with me. She has taught me to trust in God.

My prayers to Mary concerning practical matters have brought me money, beautiful houses, free airplane upgrades, good hotel rooms, the perfect car, physical protection, and guidance when I am lost. She has also offered all these things to the many people who have sought her advice through me.

In physical form, she has been my mother and my sister in other lifetimes. I remember being with her when, as the mother of Jesus, she died. I remember sharing with her the magic and mysteries of priestesshood. I remember the joys and sorrows of our lives together. She says that I am her, and I understand the essence of her message to be that we are all her and we are all God.

In the following pages she will speak directly to you . . .

INTRODUCTION

Who am I? I am the light of love. I am the spark of knowing. I am the beauty that you behold and the light that you see in one another's eyes. I am one who comes now to the Earth to speak to the hearts and minds of those who will listen, who call me, who ask that I be present with them. This is a time of tremendous momentum, with the Earth moving into the future at a pace more rapid than in the past 500,000 years. Hence, there is much taking place. I am drawn here as a magnet to support and hold the Earth in its manifestation of beauty and growth. I am also a spirit that comes to speak individually to those who wish to communicate with me. I speak in dreams. I speak in prayer. I speak in daydreams. I speak in hope. I speak in faith. I speak in trust. I speak in love.

Yes, if you wish, you may ask me to be with you and you will feel my warmth and love. The only reason you may not sense my presence would be that you do not believe I am with you. You may ask for my assistance and you will find small miracles taking place before your eyes. These are not miracles in *my* eyes. These are only the phenomena of love manifesting in the physical world.

What is a miracle? A miracle is a truth—a truth that you and I and God are one. When you ask in truth for a miracle, if it is possible and ordained by God your wish will take place. Not even I know the will of God. However, I act in accordance with this will, which can move with great force. Even heavy stones weighing tons can be moved as the will of God comes forth into your world.

I am indeed one who has walked upon the Earth in different forms—as man, as woman, even as reptilian—and I shall do so in the future. The greatest way that I can serve God in your world now is as a spirit that ventures into the hearts and minds of many. I express my being in the spirit form, in the consciousness field that is of a higher vibration than the Earth plane. You do not always know of my presence unless you open your senses of beauty and ask for it. For indeed, I am beauty. I am the beauty that you behold in all ways, and I am the love that you feel in your hearts, that you give and receive, that you open to and ask for. I am all this and more.

I come to you to assist in balancing the Earth. As each one of you is now balancing and rebalancing, so is the Earth, my most beautiful and delightful daughter. She is coming into a moment of growth, of maturing, of manifestation of her beauty and her oneness. With this balancing comes a bit of unsettledness. Each of you may feel this in different ways in your own life. You ask, "What is it that I truly believe? What is it that I truly know? What is it that I truly love?" In doing so, you will be guided more deeply into resonance and harmony with the Earth. My angelic brothers and sisters are also helping to hold the Earth in its beautiful manifestation of love.

How else do I help you? I help you as the Earth. I help you as the love that each of you feels in your heart and in the opening to this love. For when you open to love, fear dissolves, honesty settles into truth, hope flourishes in the field of trust, and beauty grows in the eyes of all. So, as you move forward step by step, moment by moment, breath by breath, as you open to love you will feel a deeper sense of peace and trust in the moments of each day and each night, and will come to understand and recognize that the presence of God is always and forever with you. When you leave the body in sleep or in fear, and finally in death, God is always present. God is the carpet on which you fly from body to body, manifestation to manifestation. God is love always and forever.

Love is real. So many of you do not believe that love is real. So many of you do not believe that love heals. You do not believe that my love is that which heals you, that your love is that which heals you, and that love of one another is that which heals you. It is as simple as that. For even if you were to venture into the realms of altered states of being, even if you were to venture into the understanding of time and space, even if you were to enter into the manifestation of form from formlessness, as magicians do, you cannot know God without love.

Those who wish to know the secrets of the universe without love will not be shown them. The knowledge will not come forth without love. So do not be afraid to love.

I'm coming to the Earth now more strongly than before, drawn as the wounds are healing, drawn as the hearts are opening, drawn as the need for balance and for bringing in the feminine vibration grows. I am here.

You ask, how can I help you? I can help you in your prayers. If you ask specifically and with an open heart, I shall answer your prayers as long as they are in accordance with God's will.

The pearl is beginning to shine within your hearts. The self wishes to be known, to be felt. The light of the self wishes to shine brightly. During this process there will be discomfort in many people's hearts and minds, for they will say, "I wish to shine forth, but I do not feel I am seen, I do not feel I am heard, I do not feel I am known." This will bring questioning, doubt, and deep sorrow that the beauty of one's self is not known. It is therefore important to communicate, to share, to open to the beauty in one another, and to open to the sincere and deeply felt desire to be known. As a result, you will often find your personal relationships moving into instability.

Allow yourselves then to recognize it is the pearl that wishes to shine, and it is the eyes that wish to see the pearl shine. These pearls are trying to find one another in your love relationships, your work relationships, your social relationships, and even your relationships with nature, the animal kingdom, and the plant kingdom. For the light is intensifying upon the Earth. The light of God, the light of truth, the force of energy is awakening the pearls so they will shine.

Do not be afraid to express your desire to shine, your desire to be known. You have so often felt you must hide, as the ostrich hides its head in the sand. Of course, you are seen, but you do not know you are seen. Now you can lift your head with pride, with glory, with a reverence for the Almighty One, and recognize that you, too, have a right to be seen, to be known, to be loved, to be in all your glory. There is room for all to shine, for all to have a place, a time, and beauty. It is important to remember this when you feel deep self-doubt and questioning and then project this doubt and questioning onto others.

Remember, it is simply the pearls that wish to shine and the eyes that wish to see the pearls. You can each imagine a pearl in your own heart and a pearl in another's heart, and your eyes looking at the other's pearl. This practice will be of great assistance.

For as you come to call upon me, as you come to know me as true within your hearts, you will begin to lose your fear. You will begin to lose the aggressive, competitive, accumulative, and self-oriented form of perception, and move into loving, honoring, and valuing your self and the selves of others as they truly are. You will see beyond the cloud of fear into the beauty, the glory of the shining brilliant luminescent pearl, the light of God, the diamond light that shines in the hearts and minds of all beings, living and nonliving.

What are the main lessons being taught upon the Earth? You are learning, first and foremost, to love, respect, honor, and embrace the self, and to love, respect, honor, and embrace God. You are learning to allow the beauty of the spirit to shine forth, and to allow this beauty to bring magnificent abundance, splendor, truth, comfort, and security. You are also learning to trust in the equality of all life, in the benefit and magnificence of abundance for all beings. You are learning to release competition and self-aggrandizement.

You have forgotten that everything carries the vibration and the glory of God. You have forgotten that God loves and God provides for all. You have forgotten that you came to Earth to learn this. I am here to remind you that the presence of God is within each of you. This is what you have come to learn. As you grow in this learning and understanding, you will find the magnificence of God's love manifesting in a physical way in your life: in beautiful surroundings, in loving relationships, in families, music, and exquisite jewels and colors.

How can you help? Each one of you can help others, as well as yourself, by seeing God in others, by seeing God in yourself, by accepting and loving one another as you fumble and struggle and fall and rise in the lessons of life. You can help by carrying one another in your hearts as beautiful beings, and by understanding that the darkness that manifests in your eyes, along with negative actions, is coming from a misunderstanding and lack of knowledge of God.

When you shine your love upon people who are in darkness, their armor and harshness begin to dissolve. You can do this by loving and accepting yourselves as

manifestations of God, with all your imperfections, which
are actually only expressions of the ignorance of God's presence. It is all there is. What you call mistakes or failures,
losses or wrongdoings are actually only little bits and pieces
of not knowing God in those moments. The more you know
the presence of God, the less these experiences occur. The
more you accept yourselves as they occur, the more you
know the presence of God.

How do I, as a spirit, heal you? I come to Earth as a healing force that you can access through your hearts, through
your hands, through your minds. I come in dreams to each
of you. I come out to those who are suffering, to offer comfort and compassion. For I love all. I see the beauty of the
love of God in everyone. I come for healing, moving different parts of the body, energizing the body, and shifting the
consciousness so that more love can enter the physical form.
I come into your minds to clarify thoughts, to bring love
and peace so the mind can work more effectively. I come
into your spirits, lightening you, freeing you, honoring and
respecting you, and loving you.

How do I heal you in your crossing over to the world of
spirit? I am simply there and you enter into my being. I hold
you dearly. I welcome you. I invite you to be with me. You
can feel me as a force of heat and love. You can feel me as a
brilliant light through which you enter into the next realm
of being. You can see me as a female figure with a magnificent gown and a skirt of light; you enter into this light. You
can see me as pure light, and feel me as the greatest force of
love you have ever known.

Before you die, you cross over many times—in sleep, in
daydreams, in loss of consciousness. Many of you, upon
reentering the Earth plane, forget that you have seen me,
been with me, heard me, felt me. But now that you hear my
voice, perhaps you will remember more often. When it is

your time, you will know that you can go peacefully in my arms, and those close to you will know this as well.

You can remember. If you listen to your hearts, use your imagination, and release your doubts, you will remember my presence. For I also assisted in your conception and entrance into the Earth plane. I and others helped to carry you into the beauty of your being, into the moment of entering that spark of life. I was there and you knew me in other ways, in other dimensions. So, you can remember now. You can see me and know that you will be with me again soon. I am present with you throughout your lives, although I come more closely in times of need, transition, and despair.

How can you be closer to me now? Call and I shall be with you. Ask and ye shall receive. Seek and ye shall find. All is well. All is true. All is love. Ask. Call to me. Pray to me. Pray in moments of fear, in moments of despair, in moments of glory, in moments of wonder. Ask that I be with you and I shall be. Ask to see me. Ask to hear me. Ask to know me and you will feel my presence.

As for the future, my children, there is a force of love being expressed now upon the Earth and within the Earth that will help you open cracks of fear, cracks of disbelief, and cracks of dishonor to the self. Remember this: they are only cracks and beneath is the beauty and glory of God's love.

So, when you find yourselves breaking into tears, into fear, or into despair, remember the cracks in the beautiful golden eggs of your beings, which are asking for the love of God to enter and to be expressed from within, healing, opening, and glorifying the beings that you are.

There will be increased fear upon the Earth as a result of these cracks opening in the world leaders. There will be doubts expressed, and there will be confrontations emerging in strange ways upon the Earth. Those who were

xxiv The Spring of Hope

once at peace will begin to argue. Those who were once at war will begin to make peace. Those who have become fat upon the misery of others will begin to feel doubt. They will question their motivation. They will question their desire for accumulation and disturbance. Because of this, there will be an increased shift in the Earth.

You see, change need not come through great explosions and mass destruction, as has been thought at other times. It can come in the awakening of the hearts and minds of those in power, when they begin to see that what they thought was right is perhaps not in accordance with God's will, truth, and love.

There is already an awakening in the hearts and minds of some leaders. When they go to sleep and when they wake up, they are beginning to question many assumptions they thought were clear and absolute. Each one of you can assist in this, perhaps by writing to your leaders, but most importantly by utilizing prayer. Pray that the leaders will awaken to the love of God and the love of truth, to the honor and respect of the Earth as a living being, to my presence in the Earth plane, and to my presence in the hearts and minds of all who call. Pray that these leaders will awaken to the reality of their beauty within and the necessity of sharing this reality with all who walk upon the Earth. In this way the Earth need not move through physical tumult, but rather shift radically as the hierarchies transform into "lovarchies," and as misconceptions turn into conceptions of love.

Gold will soon be discovered on the surface of mountains in many places, because beings have brought it from afar to assist the Earth in an energetic and economic rebalancing. A new perception of gold will emerge. People will see it as the light of God, as the vibration of the oneness and beauty that is present within the metal itself. This knowledge, once lost, will be rediscovered.

There will be skin eruptions on many people, in reaction to the polluted air and water. These can be healed through love and attention to the heart. Physical healing is not necessary, although supplements of liquid gold, green algae, magnesium, calcium, and zinc can assist in the process.

It is most important to listen deeply to your hearts and allow your energy fields to release fear. In this way you will become protected and strengthened; the pollution will not enter into your auras and, therefore, into your bodies.

So go in peace, my children, and go in love. Know that you and I and all are one. Amen.

Chapter One
ANGELS

My beloved ones, today I will speak to you about the realms of the angels. There is much knowledge coming to the Earth now concerning the angelic realms, for these beings are most interested in the motion and birthing of the Earth that is now taking place. There is a desire in the hearts of many to understand the meaning of the angelic realms, which have previously been relegated to myths, stories, fantasies, and imaginings. More and more of the human race recognizes that angelic activity may be truly present in day-to-day living.

I will speak about the hierarchies of angels. These hierarchies move in ages, which are called "eons." An eon encompasses the experience of a being. Some beings have had more eons of experience than others. In your words, it would be "eons of time." However, in the angelic or otherworldly places of being, these are considered states of being, for there is no time in such dimensions. The realms are guided by force fields of energy such as myself. I have a realm and in this realm there are angelic forces—angelic beings who may manifest into material form at different times and places, and in different states of being.

The archangels Rafael, Michael, Uriel, Stephaniel, and Gabriel also have realms. These realms differ from my own, for they have more specific orientations to the expression of the Lord. These archangels govern—although there is no governing in our worlds, but rather being—consciousness expression in different forms and aspects. Each one of these archangels leads an army of beings, a regiment of beings, although of course there is no military force in these realms. In this orientation, they move energies as an army moves tanks, guns, soldiers, food, water, and medical supplies. While shifting and sorting energies, they orient themselves toward accomplishment of a certain goal, a certain state of being. These "states-of-being armies" are conceptualizing a new way for the military experience.

So, with our armies we bring forth consciousness in many forms, many more than you can possibly imagine. I will speak now of the forms upon the Earth, for there are angelic beings present among you now. Most do not know they are angelic, for if they did know, they would extinguish their Earth life, and with it the purpose of their being here. For this reason, the consciousness of their true being is hidden in their memory cells, thereby allowing them to enact and effect that which they have come to do.

It is not important that you wonder, "Who is an angel and where will I find angels in my life? Am I an angel? Do I know angels?" Let these thoughts go. I tell you about the angels not to awaken your curiosity about the beings with whom you live but to awaken your curiosity about the beings of the angelic realms and their purpose for coming to you.

They come as emissaries, guides, and agents of the Lord. They come to assist in the upsurgence of consciousness that is now taking place. They come to teach, to show, and to demonstrate the presence of the Lord upon the Earth. This is their one and only purpose. Their mission is to demonstrate that the Lord is truly the Lord, that the Lord is not a fantasy, or a state of imagination, or a state of manipulation, or a state of indoctrination, or a state of incrimination. The Lord is only love. It is difficult for you to understand that this is in fact the truth, that this is absolutely and totally true.

There are also angelic beings in the dimensions above and close to the Earth who watch over the Earth and each one of you. These are not angelic forms in the human body; they are angelic forms in the ethereal body. You see these angels in visions and images. In biblical stories the angels are described accurately in terms of their form, although many are multidimensional, which has not been fully described in the common literature of your world. They are known by some and will be known by more.

Now, about the angelic beings present among you . . . They have come to take you to the Lord. They have come to show you that the Lord is love. They have come to be with you in all your joy, in all your pleasure, and in all your pain—to show you that the presence of the Lord is with you always. Allow yourselves now to recognize this truth in a place within your hearts that knows everything I am speaking of at the moment. This place holds your own knowledge, memory, and experience of the presence of the Lord. When I speak to you of angels—my angels as well as other angels—know that this is true. Each one of you knows deep within that this knowledge is not new but is as ancient as the Lord, for you are the Lord since you are one with the Lord.

Remember this and remember that the angelic beings are with you every moment of your life. This is my message. There will be more to come. Amen.

Chapter Two

LISTENING

Many times if you ask yourself a question and truly listen, the answer that you seek will come forth. Perhaps you do not wish to hear this answer, or perhaps you wish to hear another answer. But you know what is true and you know what is good for you. Often, you seek truth in places of darkness. Look for the good in the dark, for indeed it is there. It is a matter of translation. In your suffering there is joy. In your pain there is love. In your loneliness there is truth.

So go forth, my small ones, and listen. Listen deeply and widely. Listen to your own hearts. Listen to the hearts of others close to you. Listen to the heart of the Earth. Listen to the hearts of the angels. Listen to the heart of God. They are all always in you.

By truly listening to one another, you can bring peace upon the Earth. For there is no dilemma that cannot be solved if you truly listen. When you truly listen, you find there is no difference; there is only love. In the seeking of love, each person has his or her own love, even those who are approaching battle. If they would take moments to truly listen, there would be no war. So you see, you have all you need within your hearts.

When you encounter warfare in your own life, sit quietly. Ask yourself, "What is the truth? What is the truth of what I hear in my own heart? What is the truth I hear in the other's heart?" The other party need not be present while you to do this. When you ask truly in your own heart to listen to another's heart, the other will hear you. The other heart will know you. You can speak one-to-the-other and speak in truth. Speak in love. And so, there shall be peace upon the Earth. Amen.

Chapter Three

THE SHADOW

ach one of you has your own experience of the Creator, the source of all being. Each one of you has your own memory of this Creator that will follow you, and has followed you, through the course of your existence. This Creator can never be annihilated. It can never be forgotten. It can never be taken from you, although some may try to rob you of it.

All that you know is present, and yet there are shadows—shadows of truth, shadows of ignorance, shadows of disbelief. They are merely shadows. If you look at the source of the Shadow, you will find the Light. There is no way this Light can disappear. There is no way you can lose your awareness of this Light. Only the Shadow attempts to dissolve this memory, for it thinks it knows how to do so. But it can never, in truth, dissolve it. The Shadow is that which you reject in yourself. The Shadow feels unworthy of the Lord's love. The Shadow ignores the truth and creates illusion. The Shadow is the force of violence and the force of judgment.

The Shadow is present, and yet it is only a shadow. The being who stands in the way of the Light, who is creating the Shadow, is the one who truly knows. When you turn to face the Shadow, you find the Light of the Shadow. You find the Light shining upon you, through you, and within you always and forevermore. Many run from the Shadow and yet the Shadow is always with them. You cannot escape the Shadow. If you run and run forever, the Shadow will always be with you. It is important to stop running, to turn and say, "Hello, Shadow. I am glad you are with me. I am glad you are here to walk with me and invite me into the intimacy of my own being, into my presence, my own lovingness, my own beingness."

What is it that you resist or fear as you turn to face the Shadow? It is only that you will discover the truth. It is as simple as this. So, you run from the truth. You run and you run. Over hill and dale you run. Yet the Shadow is always with you. When you stop running, the Shadow stands still. When you turn and face the Shadow, looking directly into the Light, you cannot see the Shadow.

There have been many violent, aggressive, destructive, life-annihilating wars fought in the name of the Shadow, although they have been said to be in the name of God. If you listen now, you will hear the voice of God within. Even God has a Shadow. You may ask, "How can the Light have a shadow?" It is there, as your Shadow is. It takes form when it is attracted to your Shadow. When your Shadow draws it close, it moves to you. It is what you call the darkness. It is what you call the negative forms. It has many names, many formations, both material and nonmaterial. Yet it is only the Shadow.

I wish to welcome each one of you and to bid you to be with your Shadow. Invite your Shadow to tea, to have a conversation, to have a meeting. Say, "Hello. I wish to know you. I am glad to know you. I am glad you are with me, for you are my teacher, my guide, my mother, my father, my being. I invite you into my home, into my bed, into my being so that we can be together and travel the journey to love, one and all." Amen.

Chapter Four
THE SWORD OF DISILLUSIONMENT

early beloved ones—and you are dearly beloved—you are truly loved. Yet so often there is the doubt, the fear, the dismissal of this love. Do not be afraid to open your hearts. Do not be afraid to bring forth the truth which is you. Do not be afraid to allow the blessings of the Lord to come to you, for this is the nature of your birth. You have been born to receive the blessings of God. Remember this and you shall know the many ways of the bountifulness and the glory of God.

I would like to speak to you about the nature of honesty. What is honesty? What is honesty in relationship to honor? What is honesty in the nature of being? What is honesty in the nature of allowing oneself to be in the full energies of love?

Now, you may say, "Well, honesty means being truthful. This is what honesty is." Yes, and so it is, and yet each one of you has difficulty being truly truthful, truly honest with yourself. When you are not honest with yourself, you live with the shadow of fear. You live with the shadow that someday someone will discover your Shadow, and this will create devastation around you. So you hide the Shadow, and yet you know deep in your heart the Shadow is present. You also know that the Shadow is only a shadow. Yet you fear that if you reveal yourself in the full light to God, to what appears to be the ultimate justice, devastation will

9

occur and you will therefore be devastated by revealing what is in fact the truth, even in the eyes of God.

In your heart you have a sword, a sword of fear. When you remove this sword, you will discover that rather than dying, the heart brings forth an increased abundance of truth.

Now, what is this sword? Dearly beloved ones, this sword is of your own making, resulting from your disorientation to the truth. This sword says, "I am who I am, and yet I do not want you to know me, so I create a mask. I create a form. I create an illusion. I create an image. I create a belief that I am one with the sword in my heart, that I must live with this sword, that I must live in pain, in suffering, in fear, in dishonesty."

You have carried this sword with you for centuries of pain, lifetimes of torture. Now it is time to remove the sword. I can remove it, if you wish. I can remove this sword so that you can live fully and truly in honesty, in honor, and in trust.

Now, this is the same sword that the archangel Michael carries in his hand to honor and enlighten all beings in the truth of the Lord. It is the sword turned outward rather than inward. So you can imagine the power of your sword. You can imagine the power of that force in your heart. It is the same force as that of Michael, for in fact he and you and I and all are one. It will take some time for you to understand this deeply.

You are, in your own heart, beginning to dislodge the sword, beginning to remove it, to loosen it, to open the heart. For it is in opening the heart that the sword is removed. It is not in pulling or forcing it out. It is only in opening, for when you open, there is no wall to hold the sword in place and the sword moves out and finds its place before you.

I would like to tell you now about the Lord. Who is the

Lord? It is a question that many ask. It is a question that even God asks. You may wonder, "How can this be? How can God ask God who God is?" God, too, has a reflection, as do you. God has a reflection that shines back and opens up to the energies of separation. The appellation that has been applied to this reflection is Evil. This reflection is only a reflection. Just as you are a reflection of your truth, so, too, is God a reflection of God's truth.

You may ask, "Well, how is it that God is one and there is a reflection present that creates two?" It is not two, just as you are not two. Actually, a reflection is merely an image given back and the eyes looking upon it see it as an image. If the eyes looking upon it see it as an aspect of that which is reflected, there is no perception of an image. God and God's reflection is like the light of the Sun and the Moon that reflects this light. Moonlight, as you know it, is an extension of the aura, or energy field, of the Sun, which on its own bathes the Earth, nourishing, healing, opening, and blessing. It is the same for you.

So, this sword in your heart is the reflection of the light, of the love of the Lord. It is an illusion. If you wish it to remain, you can keep it present within your heart. If you remove it, there will be an alteration within you forevermore. In your *wish* to be free of the sword in your heart, you are stepping forward into a new light. You are stepping forward to freedom. You are stepping forward to truth. You are stepping forward to love. You are stepping forward to your own being that's calling.

Dearly beloved ones, you are loved by God. You are God. You are only and completely God. As you remove this sword, you will *know* that you are God. Perhaps you will forget or have already forgotten. Perhaps you will never forget. Whether you remember or forget does not matter, for God's love is happening nonetheless. It is with you always and forevermore. When you remove the sword from your heart, you assist every other human being, living and non-living, in removing their swords as well.

If you are willing now, I will assist. I will bring forth the light of the Lord to assist you in removing this sword. It is possible to be fully present now, attending to the delicacy of your beautiful heart. Attend now to your heart. If you wish the sword to be removed, ask God to remove it and it shall be done. I will give you a moment of time, time in your world, to choose if you wish to release your sword.

Now, my children, be in peace. Be in the glory that you are. Be in the nature of honesty that you are. Be in the blessedness of God. You are one. Remember this: there is no difference between you and me and God and one another. The Lord is one and one is all. Amen.

Chapter Five

OVERCOMING
CHALLENGES
THROUGH LOVE

y children, I am delighted to be among you now so that the presence of my being may encourage each of you to recognize the beauty that dwells within you, the beauty of your own self, the beauty of your own thoughts, the beauty of your own heart, the beauty of your own being as it lives in the body. For indeed, you are dwelling only momentarily upon the Earth. Your self will then move forward into other dimensions. It inhabits the body in order to learn the nature of love. Learning the nature of love is indeed the greatest challenge upon the Earth.

Each of you, in your own way, is learning about love and learning how to meet the challenges that are presented to you in relation to love. It is easy to learn about love in other forms, without a body. It is more difficult to learn about love in a body that lives in continual fear that it will no longer be, that it will die. Because of this fear of death, it is more difficult to learn to love. But as you do, you alter the forms your soul has gathered as moss on a rock. You begin to move faster, allowing the boat of your self to flow more easily, and the love then acts as a lubricant for the flow. In this way, you are giving your soul a great opportunity to meet the challenges of love and to move forward, so that when you face your death you will do so with great joy and recognition of the value and truth of love.

Love is one who wears many clothes. Love comes garbed in a variety of dresses, suits, shirts, ties, shoes, and hats. You will find that you, in your lovingness of your own self, whatever the attire may be, can open the hearts of those who come close to you.

So many people think they must love only from a distance. Some love only once or just briefly. Some love only if you act in a certain way, or if you achieve what they expect of you, or if you are sweet and gentle. In your loving, you can melt these conditions. You can erode misunderstandings about love and open the hearts of others by merely opening your own heart. It is not that you must tell them something, or show them something, or ask something, or be silent. You need only open your heart and love them, appreciating them beneath their fear and their pain—and beneath their efforts to hide their loving.

You are each learning these lessons rapidly and with great fervor and honesty. It is a delight to see this manifesting in your lives. You do not yet know, although you will soon, about the seeds you have planted and how they shall grow. Many seeds will be growing now, and many forms of glorification will come to you. At times you will be surprised to be honored in such a way. You will ask, "But what did I do?" I shall answer, "You opened your heart and let the love flow through you. That is all you did."

Many times you may not know where your love flows. You may not know the ways in which your voice and your gaze are received, the differences your touch has made. Yet many ripples take place as a result of these small acts of love.

So, do not be afraid to love. Do not worry that your love is not known and felt, for indeed it is. Many times this may not be shown to you, for it is not time for you to know.

Often you look for a response from someone else, rather than trust that your love is indeed love, pure love, and that it is felt and known, even though the response is not apparent. If you focus only on the desired response, you may become drawn into the anticipation and forget how to love. You may forget that the flow of love is what brings that seed to be planted. What matters is the flow *from* you, not *to* you. If you can remember this is a cyclical force, it will be a great blessing to you in the future. You will see always that love brings forth love, and yet when you expect it, you can place a barrier between you and the response to your love.

Yes, my children, there will be challenges in your lives. There already are and there shall be more. It is not that you are alone in these challenges; nor are you wrong if you experience them. It is a commonplace misconception upon the Earth—a most devastating misconception—that when things do not go as well as might be expected, one has done something wrong. It is not so. It is most important to recognize this. Each challenge is simply an opportunity to learn how to love, to trust, to believe, to have faith, and most of all and most deeply, to love the beautiful self that lives within you.

So, do not be afraid when things go wrong. Do not be afraid that you have erred, for a challenge is an act of God. It is a creation of you and the Lord, one and the same, creating another opportunity to go forward in love, in truth, and in the blessing of all that is. You might consider it a strengthening—not a strengthening to be so strong and so tough and so distant from an event, but a strengthening to believe in yourself, in your choices, in your decisions. A strengthening to believe in your love, your vision, your dreams, your hopes, and your faith.

Go forth, my children, and do not be afraid when things go askew. It is merely an invitation to love. Amen.

Chapter Six

THE FORCE
OF CHANGE

Dearly beloved ones, another wave of force is entering into the Earth's energy field. This intensity will increase the desire to change, to move beyond current restrictions, to bring forth the energy of your heart. You will not return to the status quo or state of being of the past. No, this will never occur again. You will be catapulted into a new wave. If you resist, you will be hurt, for any resistance to change is painful. Remember this. Remember it deeply and dearly within your hearts, for each one of you has fought to remain static in the security of knowing, holding on to what is familiar and fixed.

Now, of course, there is no such thing as a fixed form, for change is ongoing. So, you are finding yourselves energized, mobilized to move beyond the present motion in your lives, beyond the present attachments, beyond the present alienations. You will be reaching out to others, joining others, bonding with one another, bonding in your hearts.

You are replacing the restrictions of love with connection, bonding, and holding the hearts of one another. The alienation, aloneness, frustrations, resentments, angers, doubts, and fears—all of this you can leave behind in one swoop of your eyes. One glance and it is gone. This glance is into your own being to find the golden light that is present there and to trust in the Lord. More than anything else, trusting in the Lord and receiving the love of the Lord must be your focus. This will hold you safe beyond all else. It will hold you in reverence of the union of all that is above all else. You will soon see that this is the most valuable treasure that you can hold, forever and ever, past, present, and future.

You can no longer deny the growth that is taking place within you. If you do, you will extinguish this growth, and you may even extinguish yourselves. Instead, you must honor this growth. It is like a growing plant. If you cut the stem, you will kill the plant. If you deny your growth, you will kill the light within your bodies.

These are strong words. These are words that will touch you deep in your hearts if you allow them to. These are words that speak profoundly to the knowledge and wisdom that is within you. For each of you knows this without a doubt, and yet you fight and scream in agony to prevent this growth from taking place. It is as if you wish to be in the darkness, convinced by the illusion that this is where to find safety. No, the safety is in the light. The safety is in the Lord. The safety is in the holding of others dearly and belovedly in your hearts, in your arms, in the depth of your souls.

Remember that God loves you dearly, and the love of God and God's love is your light. You are this light. You are no different from God. God is you; you are God. There is no difference. You are me; I am you; you are one another. There is no difference. The light is all that is. As you come to realize this, you will find a great joy blooming in your hearts. Remember, joy is wherever you are, for joy is the light, love, and union with all that is.

As you venture forth into your lives, into your homes, into your daily work and your daily thoughts, remember the light is always with you. Remember you are always with the light. You may imagine this light as the most beautiful, brilliant, effervescent light of love—perhaps a sun, for the Sun is the closest you can come in the physical human experience to imagining this light. Its intensity is the closest you can come to imagining the glory of the light of the Lord.

So, when you look upon the Sun and receive its nourishing and healing rays, think about the Lord as being multifold suns, so intense that you cannot imagine it in its reality. Only in the depth of your souls do you know this. The light comes softly to you, gently. The glory of the Lord is a gentle, loving love. It is completely and wholly love. There is nothing but love.

So, when you look upon the Sun, imagine deep within the Golden Sun beyond all else—the Golden Sun that holds all that is. In this way, you will be reminding yourself of this Golden Sun, this presence of light.

I am among you. I am with you. I am in many places upon the Earth now, to manifest a belief in the Lord; to activate faith, hope, and charity; to bring forth the love and respect of each being, living and nonliving, upon the Earth. All is with God. God is with all.

When you are with this Sun of the Lord, the details of your lives fall gently into place in new forms, as if you threw the pieces up and they landed in a new pattern. In trust and faith you can move forward through a pattern that works more easily in all ways for you. It is more smooth and peaceful, more gentle, more nourishing, more loving, and more in accordance with your own desires, your own truth, your own love.

So, remember this and throw the pieces up. Let go of all you have created until now, and allow the pieces to take a new form, a new configuration. All of what you have planned will be disrupted. All of what you have organized will be disturbed, unable to take place as you have visualized. I tell you this now with love and respect for your intentions and your desire for order in the chaos, for clarity in the obscurity, and for joy in the darkness. Let go now. All that you have planned, each one of you, let it go. Let it sail high upon the waves of love back to the Lord. Let the Lord feed and nourish it. Release it all. For none of what you have planned, organized, or imagined will take place in keeping with the expectations you have in mind at this time.

Enjoy love. Enjoy spontaneity. Enjoy the beauty of the creation of the Lord. Let it be. Let it be so. Bring blessings to your heart. Bring joy. Bring love and the pleasure of being together. Release all expectation, all attachment to a form of living that is no longer applicable. Release it. Allow it to be in the presence of the Lord. Trust in the love. For all that is around you and with you, far and close, is of the Lord, is of love.

Let your souls express your deepest desires and you will find that the Lord shines forth from your souls. You shall know the course to take. You shall know the way and you shall bring together all that you love. But know also that the pieces will fly up again and again, causing the forms to continually change. Allow it to be and allow for a two-week period each time the pieces are released to bring forth a new design, a new structure. The linear way, the rigidity of the linear form, the structures, the hierarchies, the building upon building upon building will all dissolve. So, allow it to be.

I am always with you. There will be times when all you know is that I am with you. All you can rely on is my being, the being of the Lord, the being of your hearts, and the being of your love. Allow it to be, for it is the glory and the joy of the greatest gift you can receive—the love and the presence of God.

So, my children, remember I am always with you. You can call upon me in any moment. Call me by name. Ask if I am there. Ask, "Are you there, Mary? Are you there, Mother? Are you there, Divine Goddess?" Call me whatever name you wish. I shall answer and I shall be with you, as I am always. Amen.

Chapter Seven
GOLD

reed is a dimensional force upon the Earth that has created much suffering and much pain, both for those in greed and for those from whom the greedy have taken.

There is a sacred law that says, "You shall be given all that you need to live in beauty and truth and joy and comfort and peace. You shall be given all that you ask for." Yet there are many who continue to accumulate, who do not create beauty and joy and peace and love and comfort for themselves and those they love. They move far beyond, disconnected from their own selves, disconnected from their own beauty, their own joy, and their own comfort.

It is in this disconnection that greed enters. It is not greedy to want to live in beauty, even in affluence, for the sake of beauty and comfort and peace. You can have all that you wish for in this way. However, when you lose connection to the beauty, the joy, the comfort, and the security within you, and you strive to accumulate mountains and mountains of gold and silver, buildings, and stocks and bonds, there is an imbalance. Each one of you is moving through a major transition, which is creating a huge upheaval, a significant opening, a bursting through of joy, love, and the ecstasy of living in beauty, truth, comfort, and peace.

So you ask yourselves, "How can I create this balance within? How can I bring forth the resources I need in order to create this state of being for myself and those I love and care for? How can I move the resources I have into the dimensions of balance and contribution and dedication to what I believe in most dearly, which is the love of the Lord, the love of beauty, the love of security, the love of peace, and the love of joy?"

It is not wrong to be greedy. It is not wrong to accumulate mountains and mountains of gold and silver. If you wish to share the mountains of gold and silver with others to create beauty and joy and security and peace, you will find a great sense of connection to your own self and to the joy of being one with the Lord. If you disconnect from yourself and begin to focus on the mountains of gold and silver, you will become lost sheep. You will not know the Lord. You will not know the truth, the security, the joy, and the peace that you seek and that you seek to create for others. You will feel alone and you will be afraid of dying. You will bring only further aloneness and separation.

There is a movement now upon the Earth that requires rebalancing. The places of need are so large and the consciousness of the planet is becoming so strong that resources are pouring into these places of need. Many times they are misused, consumed by the greed of others in the name of caring, in the name of help, and in the name of truth. This also will be rebalanced soon. It is important to understand that an entire reassessment and realignment of resources is now taking place upon the Earth.

There will be tremendous resistance to this. There will be wars fought over this, but remember that it is a balancing of resources. It is not a taking away or a giving. It is a balancing, a sharing. It is like water flowing to where it is most needed.

Do not be afraid if you are confused about this. Indeed, most beings upon the Earth are quite confused about it at this moment in time. There is a disturbance of the status quo, and you will find, more and more, in the stock market, in the energies of land, and in the energies of gold itself that a realignment is already taking place.

Consider very carefully how and where you put your resources, and what it is that you wish to enhance first in your life. Consider your home, your family, your surroundings, your clothes, your jewelry, your books, your living space, your land, your automobile, your food, your friends. Alterations are taking place in all dimensions. It is important to know that you will always live in beauty, joy, and peace if you so wish.

At times you may feel your space threatened, but do not be concerned. You will know how to sift and sort through the resources. You will know whom to assist and who can assist you. You will know, in the bottom of your hearts, in the deepest place of your hearts, what is correct and what is not. You will find, more and more, that you must rely on your own truth, your own love, your own desire, and your sense of harmony and balance.

Gold is a symbol of the Golden Sun, the son of God, the great Central Sun, God, the Lord. As you allow gold to flow, you will find that the flow will bring you increasing joy and peace. For you will know that you are guided in the expression of the flow.

Allow the wonderings, imaginings, and intuitive glimpses of the future to remain in your consciousness. You are creating now. You are creating the future. You are creating your lives. You are creating the flow of gold. You are creating the flow of love. For yourselves, first and foremost, for the dear beloved selves that you are, for the divine beings that you are, let the gold be a joyful expression of you. Let yourselves shine in golden light. Let the gold flow through your veins, healing and lightening you, to bring forth the essence of your truth and your love. Let it flow for you and with you.

From this golden light, you shall bring forth the fruits of the gold in the world around you, for yourselves and for those you love and hold precious. Let the gold flow to those you love and care for.

Remember, the Temple is within. The Golden Temple is you. The Golden Temple is that which is of your essence in the nature of the union with God, with the Lord, and with all that is.

So, my children, my beloved ones, remember that all is well within, that all is in truth and all is holy. Remember that gold is holy. Remember that you are holy. Remember that the love of the Lord is the holy sacrament of truth. Remember that you are that which you seek. You are that which you love. You are that which is. Amen.

Chapter Eight
MONEY

y children, upon the Earth now are many occurrences that will bring forth fear. More and more of these will be taking place, sometimes subtly, sometimes more obviously. For there is a motion deep within the Earth to heal, to be known, and to be righted into balance. You have already felt it. There may be an uncomfortableness at times when you walk upon the streets, when you go to sleep at night, when you meet somebody, when you go to a party, when you meditate, or when you are in an embrace. You may have moments of fluttering fears. This is the sensitivity that you are developing for the transmutation of fear.

More and more, the fear will be felt economically. When fear erupts as a result of the constriction and alteration of economics, it causes an increase in rage that brings forth more rage.

So walk softly, dearly, and in truth. You may have an inkling of the fear, perhaps a tension, a sense of danger, a feeling of awakening to the truth. There has been much repression, distortion, violation, and aggression forced upon many people of the world. This will no longer be tolerated. Even the oppressors will begin to feel an opening.

Acknowledge deeply and profoundly the truth as you know it, and when you feel ready begin to speak it, to write it, and to otherwise communicate it. It is in the communication of truth that communion takes place. Communion is the union of the physical and nonphysical worlds. It is the union of matter and spirit. It is the union of all beings and all forms into the formless oneness of God.

At times you choose not to speak the truth, at least not to speak it in certain circles for fear that those circles will contract rather than expand. You wish not to bring such pain upon yourselves. So choose where and with whom to speak that which you hold to be dearest and truest. You will know in your hearts when it is wise to speak and when it is not, and at moments you may find yourself in the middle of a sentence, then stop and say, "No. No more. I will not go further."

Each of you has experienced the suffering that comes from economic dependency. Each of you has felt the fears, the pain, and the tears brought on by the phenomenon of money. If you consider money an expression of joy and truth, it will bring you joy and truth. If you regard it as a burden, you will find it becoming more of a burden. Think of it as a phenomenon separate from yourselves—an exchange of energy, an exchange of light. It is not you. You are not the money. You are not the bank account. You are not the dollar bill. You are not the goods or services that come your way as a result of this exchange.

Remember that you exist and shall exist far beyond the coins, far beyond the paper and the ink and the bills, far beyond all goods you can obtain and all goods you can give. When you shift your focus away from the economic material force and toward yourselves, you will find that you can love money and be loved by it.

I speak now, for there is much fear that will emerge and has already emerged upon the Earth. When you can walk with no fear of economics, no fear of money, no fear of intrusion, abandonment, or exclusion as a result of the money, you will find great happiness bursting forth in your hearts. You will also find that you will be able to assist others, many others, in the management and organization of consciousness in relationship to money.

Remember, each one of you, do not fear your own heart, for it is the guiding light of God that shines. Do not fear your own heart with all its wishes and desires, its knowings and truths, and its capacity to bring forth love and join with another, or many others. There are hearts waiting to join yours, to pulsate and throb in the presence of yours. Do not fear this, for it is the greatest glory you can bring upon yourself. Amen.

Chapter Nine
ALLIANCES

early beloved ones, I am present among you to bring forth the message of love: love of our Lord, love of your Lord, love of the Lord. I am here also to remind you of the energies of truth, that when you look within, you will find the light of love, and that the darkness you see in the mirror is only an illusion. And yet, this darkness is a presence you must confront in order to move forward, to cleanse and purify that which you are. In the essence of your being, there is truth. At the bottom of the well you will find the truth if you look deeply into your reflection in the water. The truth will not always be that which you wish to find, but it will be the gold that you discover. It is here now for you to honor and to bring forth, each in your own way.

I come, too, to remind you of the formation of the energies of alliance. There are many alliances taking place now upon the Earth—in personal ways, in energetic ways that are not yet personalized, in national ways, in global ways, in ways with other beings from other dimensional existences, and among those beings. These alliances create energy lines upon the Earth. The energy lines assist in the formation and the balancing of emerging alliances with other planets and with other beings on the Earth itself. It is as if, in entering into an alliance, you are creating, in conjunction with all these forces, new acupuncture points upon the Earth. Very soon you may be drawn to other lands in order to reestablish these alliances—some of which you have known in the past as well as the new ones you will be bringing forth. These alliances will then solidify and magnify, bringing you into your energy fields. The alliances within you are taking place with your spirit guides, with your memory cells, and with physical and nonphysical beings you will be bringing forth in the future.

You are all creations and you are continually creating. Amid this creative force, you are aligning your energies with one another. You are creating alliances. Now, this connection may break or extend itself, or it may solidify and gradually form an acupuncture point.

You are creating many acupuncture points not only within the spatial dimensions you are connected to but also within the Earth, and within the spatial dimensions now entering the Earth's energy fields. All these networks are being arranged, shall we say, in such a way as to bring forth the magnitude of love needed to take the Earth into its birthing emergence. So it is that each one of you may wish to consider the desire you have in your heart to travel, the desire you have in your heart to speak to those who are next door, in another city or state, in another country, even to those who have moved on to other dimensions. All these alliances are realigning, reconnecting in new networks of Light.

You are here to bring forth an expression of this Light. You will carry Light with you into the next moments of your lives, and also carry these alliances with you. The alliances you have established in the past—relationships, as you call them—are dissolving rapidly. They are dissolving in order to realign in new ways. Some of them will be continuing and some will not. There is no judgment here. There is no force of will. You are both creator and created, continuing with the love and alignment balancing all the forces that surround and interpenetrate the Earth and surround and interpenetrate your own being. So go forth, my children, in love and alliance. Be at peace. Amen.

Chapter Ten
DNA Shifts

early beloved children, there are many times in your lives when you feel lonely. You feel as though God is not real, there is no truth, no reliable reality, no honesty, no improvement. You feel only despair and uncertainty. You ask, "Is this life? Am I alive? Am I true? Am I present in my body? Am I honest in my mind and my heart? Am I one who lives or am I one who only appears to live? What is the meaning of life?" Many questions arise; many answers disperse into the oneness, lost to the mind.

In a single moment you exist now, forever, and beyond. You ask, "How can that be? How can it be that I am only one and yet one with all? How can it be that I am in union and yet single, separate, and alone? How can two states of being exist, one with another, in the same moment of time?"

Allow yourselves to imagine that time moves beyond what you know of it at the moment, that time is merely a construct of the mind, that time is only what you believe it to be. In this way you will find yourselves able to transcend time, and be without time. Many of you have wondered, "Why must I be a captive of the moment? Why must I be only in this moment? Why can't I be in many moments simultaneously?" Indeed, you can.

There is a form of evolution taking place in your DNA, in your chromosomes, in all your nerves, in all your organs, and in your brains. You are living within the moment of movement into the future and the past.

Your metabolism is accelerating at a rapid rate, moving your consciousness into expansiveness and multidimensional time. It will not slow down. There is a tendency for you to wish or even believe that this is momentary. It is not. But if you allow your consciousness to speak and your hearts to open to the wisdom that is passing through you, you will find yourselves expanding in truth and destroying falsehood.

Today's increase in allergic reactions is due to the intensification of winds, the changing DNA of plants, and the escalating pollution and distortion of energy fields. Such allergic reactions will multiply. If you wish, you can absorb the energies of vitamins, the energies of the sea, and the energies of the rocks. These will assist you in maintaining an equilibrium.

Weather patterns are shifting—temperatures are changing, winds are altering. The frigid and torrid zones are shifting slightly. The land of the Southwest will gradually sink. If you periodically measure the land mass above water, you will find it is decreasing. The sinking, due to shifts that are taking place deep within the Earth, will continue.

Do not be frightened. Only be aware, become sensitive to your emotions as they respond to these slight changes. Even a millimeter of change in dimensional space can affect your consciousness. It is important that you notice the change. You might say to yourself, "Ah, I feel something moving. I feel a greater pressure. I feel a slight instability I cannot explain. I feel a change."

Listen. Watch. Wait. Observe the animals and the birds. Notice the plants. Pay attention to the friends that live in the sea. Listen to the winds. So often you dismiss the value of sound and its impact. Each one of you will begin to reach beyond the walls of your home, beyond the boundaries of your city, beyond the borders of your state. You will begin to reach into new lands and explore new territory. You will start to ask yourself more deeply, "What is it that I have come to do and why am I not doing it? What is it that I want and how do I stop myself from wanting it? What is it that I love and why am I afraid to love? What is it that I know and why I am afraid to know?"

Even without asking the questions, you will find the answers. The early morning hours are excellent for awakening to the truth, as are the midday hours. Notice at midday, between noon and 2:00 p.m., the lull in the energy force; this is a time to rest and to listen. Listen, my children, listen to what you hear and what you wish to hear. Ask in your hearts, "Do I hear what it is I truly wish to hear or do I hear what I believe I must hear?" Ask, "What changes can I make in my life in order to hear what it is I truly wish to hear? Do I wish to hear these vibrations within my eardrum?"

There is much ahead in each of your lives—much exploration, adventure, breaking through walls you have built around yourselves, breaking through bombshells you live in or believe you live in, breaking through sadness, love, falsehood, blindness. So go forward into your own knowledge and with the blessing of all that you are. Amen.

Chapter Eleven
BEYOND COMPUTERS

early beloved children, I come to you in order to assist you in the alteration of your perceptions. Your perceptions are limited by that which you believe to be true.

There are many forces present among you that you are not aware of in your conscious minds. These forces are waiting for you to know them. They are spirits of the Earth, spirits of the plants, spirits of the trees, spirits of the rocks and the soil, spirits of the birds, spirits of places, and spirits of the angelic realm of which I am a part. They are beings who have passed on, who wish to be a part of the glorious events about to take place. These beings have participated in the past motion of the Earth and are most eager and excited to be a part of this change. All these beings are waiting for each of you to make their acquaintance.

Many times they come to you in dreams and in visions that you do not consciously register. For instance, you may be looking at a tree and the spirit of the tree comes forth to meet you. You do not see this spirit with your physical eyes, but your brain records its presence. There are many capacities within your cellular system that you have not yet realized. They are, as you might say, hidden in the closet and waiting for the day the closet door will open. These spirits are quite alive, quite vibrant in light, quite wise in the messages they have to give you, and they are waiting for you to meet them.

Some doors are opening to your perceptions now. At

times they open and then immediately close. You see gold or blue light, but you do not consciously record this perception. You see hues of light that are not encoded in your color system. As a result, you do not know you are seeing them. You hear voices, but you do not know you are hearing them. The cells in your brain are monitoring these sensations, and all the while collecting information. The seeds have been planted and are waiting for the water and the sun to awaken them.

Your DNA coding is shifting as a result of these expanding perceptions. The cellular influences that affect the DNA coding are triggering a shift in understanding and attunement that will enable you to pass through the momentum of the Earth's energy shift. As you pass through this shift, you will be receptive to the forces that are presently entering the Earth's energy field. For this reason, you may be tired. It is a time to rest, to minimize your activities, to allow the structure of the cells to alter. The nuclei of the cells need to open and the cells need to fly free so that they can align with this intensified electrical force field.

This force field will allow you to perceive new colors and even perform miracles, such as walking on water. It will also allow you to telepathically communicate across global communication systems—to communicate mountain to mountain, spanning the globe with no technological support. This force field will further enable you to access new healing methods, new awakening techniques, new forms of physical expression, and new ways to communicate with other-dimensional forces. Your perceptions will change. You will see the new colors. You will hear the new voices. You will see new beings. Of course, these are not new, but they will be new to you.

The new communication methods will extend to daily life. Hence, rising above the matrix of technological-

electrical force is important now. Technological communications have created a bit of pollution upon the Earth, a bit
of confusion in the Earth's intelligence, a bit of disturbance
in the heart of the Earth. This is not negative or wrong; it is
a part of the evolution of human consciousness. For this
reason, it is needed and valued. If you so wish, you can
move beyond these systems. Rather than communicate
through your computers, communicate through your hearts
and through the inner ear. You will indeed be able to hear
one another in this way. You will also be able to decide
when and how to invest in the stock market. You will know
when and how to communicate with your family. You will
know when and how to send a message of love to one who
is in pain. You will know when and how to step forward in
your work. The only reason you have not yet progressed
beyond technologically supported communication systems
is that you have not taken the moment to sit quietly and ask
about this form of communcation.

All that you use your computers for you can do with
your minds. In fact, the mind moves much faster than the
computer. It also connects to other dimensions more easily
and rapidly. Therefore, if you so choose, you may transcend
the computer and move into your own wisdom. For now
you may wish to continue using the computer to communicate with the outer world. You may opt to continue relying
on microchips in your daily lives. I wish only to suggest that
there is another way of knowing, another way of communicating, another way of expressing.

I offer you this opportunity to expand and activate your
own capacities, your own brain cells. To do so, you need
only open the doors of the closet and release the forces of
wisdom and intelligence that you hold in all the cells of
your bodies. This will strengthen the cells of your nervous
systems.

So go forth, my children. Go forth in your wisdom. Go forth in your knowledge. Go forth in your capacity to grow. Go forth in your capacity to love. Go forth in your capacity to create truth. In this way you can alter the future. And so it is so. Amen.

Chapter Twelve
MIRACLES

o, my beloved children, you are wondering why it is that you have chosen to be in the human form at this time. Why is it that you have decided to be present during a time when the Earth is moving into a new form? It is a question that is in each of your hearts, although it may not always be present in your conscious minds.

Many forces that you are confronting wish you to lose your way. Each one of you in your own heart knows already the forces that strive to prevent your forward motion. They are what you are experiencing when you say, "I do not want to do this," or "I'm too tired to do this," or "It seems too difficult to do this," or inside you find a voice of "no" when you want to say "yes," or perhaps you find a tear coming to your eyes when you say "yes."

Each moment that you say, "I can," "I will," "Yes," the way opens. This is precisely how the Red Sea opened to the followers of God. It is the way miracles have taken place in your history. Each one of you can create miracles. Each one of you can create a gift of God through your own hands, with your own voice, with your own eyes. But very often you do not believe this is possible. You do not believe you are a miracle worker. You believe you are instead a victim of circumstance.

As you look within your hearts, beloved ones, you will know that there is truth to what I say. If you look carefully and listen, you will see miracles taking place each day in your own lives. If you look back through the years, you will recognize miracles you have created. It is important, my children, that you realize you are the creators. Understand this: the world is that which you create. Your visions, your images, your thoughts are all creators. And beyond these, the greatest creator is your love.

Do not be afraid to step forward and say, "I can create miracles." It is the secret of magic. It is the secret of creation. It is the manifestation of God. As you step forward in your lives, with each breath that you take ask in your hearts for the honor of being a creator of Earth, a creator of heaven on Earth, a creator of all that is. For there is no difference between you and the one that is the great Creator, the Creator of all, the Lord of all, the Lord of love, the Lord of truth, the Lord of honor, the Lord of respect. You are no different from the Lord of all. You have simply chosen a different form, just as you have chosen a form different from a tree, an automobile, a piece of candy, the dirt on the street. All the same, yet different. Amen.

Chapter Thirteen

AGING
AND AWARENESS

early beloved ones, I come to speak to you concerning the energy of awareness. Awareness is the result of becoming conscious, of becoming actively alert in the force fields of energy around you. To become aware is to become alive—alive with all the cells actively expressing life force, alive with creation, alive with activation, alive in the expression of truth, and alive in the excitement, pleasure, and joy of being alive.

In this state there is no aging. There is no wear and tear upon the body, no wear and tear upon the cells. There is only joyful living. It is a way you can continue your lives for many years until at some point you may decide, "I wish to rest now" or "I wish to make a transition to another dimension." Then you will rest or make the transition.

So, awareness is aliveness. In this state of aliveness there is an activation of connection to other alive energies—live wires, so to speak. In connecting to these energies, you increase your aliveness. Technically, you are alive until you die. However, each one of you has placed walls in different orientations to obstruct your aliveness, to obstruct the full joy and beauty of the aliveness of that which you are.

So go forward, my children, into the beauty and the glory of life, and know that you and I and all are one. Amen.

Chapter Fourteen

THE NATURE
OF GOD

early beloved children, you ask what it is that you have come to do upon the Earth. You ask to know if the presence of God is of you, if the presence of God is all around you, if you and God and all are one.

Each of you has stepped forward now to say, "Yes, I am here. Yes, I am real. Yes, I am honored. Yes, I am loved." For you would not have walked to Earth through the door of love unless you knew somewhere in your heart that you were indeed loved by God. It is that knowledge that brings you to the oneness of God. It is that knowledge that takes you on the path to God. It is that knowledge that takes you to the truth of God. So, as you walk now in your life, you will never again forget that God walks with you as you, that you walk with God, that you know God. Your mind may ignore these words, but your heart knows that what I speak of is true.

And so, it is in this way that you can walk in the world knowing that the love of God is always with you. When you transit from this world to the next, you will find that God is with you. When you are suffering, crying in pain, sadness, distortion, or loneliness, you will know within your heart, within your soul that the love of God is with you. When you remember this, you will feel the strength of God's love. When you do not remember it, God's love will still be with you. It is only that you will not have allowed yourself to feel the strength of this love. Because of this strength, you can do many things you do not think are possible. There are many adventures ahead that will allow you to know God's presence is always with you in your heart, always holding you, and always loving you.

You may ask, "What is God? Who is God? Where is God?" God is the presence of love, simply and only this. Whenever you love, however you love, whomever you love, that is God, that is God's love. As you walk and open your hearts to love, you will find God more and more with you. It is only that you do not recognize this. So, as you walk through your lives, through the presence of the Lord you will find more and more love and feel more and more the presence of God. You may say, "Oh no, God must be a figure of importance, must be a powerful presence, a being that sits in greatness of all that occurs." Actually, God is only love. It is as simple as this. I come to you to teach that God is only love.

There are many ways that love flows to expression in the physical world. There are many ways in each moment of your lives that love is present within you. This love extends both to people with whom you have close contact and to those at a distance. So, then, how do you walk knowing that God is with you? You listen. You listen to your hearts and your hearts will bring forth this truth. You do not need to seek it outwardly. You do not need to read books, watch movies, listen to music, or even meditate or pray. All of these are pathways to the heart, yet it is in your hearts that you will find God.

Each of you has a most beautiful heart and a most loving heart. It is something that will always be with you. As you move through time and space, your heart is constantly with you. The sacred heart—that is what it is. The heart knows. The heart is what speaks the words of love and the words of God.

Your own heart knows. You do not need to look else-where—above, below, this way or that. Only sit quietly and listen. All that you wish to take place, all that you wish to know, all that you wish to feel, all that you wish to discover is within you. You will know this if you listen. In the listening you will find your world beginning to take on new forms, new shapes, new colors, new feelings, new sensations, new thoughts, new memories, and new awakenings, all within the moment of the heart. So be at peace, my children, and in love, and know that you and I and all are one. Amen.

ABOUT THE AUTHOR

Carolyn E. Cobelo, MSW, is a spiritual teacher and a leader of spiritual pilgrimages to sacred places around the world. An ordained minister in the Church of the Living God, she has practiced spiritual psychology for twenty-five years. Her extensive personal experience in passing through major life transitions assists her in creating deeply moving ceremonies and celebrations.

Founder and director of the School of Akashic Evolution in New York and in Buenos Aires, Argentina, Carolyn has taught seminars in North and South America, Europe, and the Middle East. She is presently the director of Akasha Institute and Alcyon Sacred Arts Alliance in Santa Fe, New Mexico, as well as an artist, designer, composer, and mother of three children. Her published works include *The Power of Sacred Space: Exploring Ancient Ceremonial Sites; Awakening to Soul Love: Pathways to Intimacy; Twenty-Five Power Places;* and *Avalon: The Temple of Connection,* a board game.